Make Your Own
Puppets

Anna-Marie D'Cruz

PowerKiDS
press.

New York

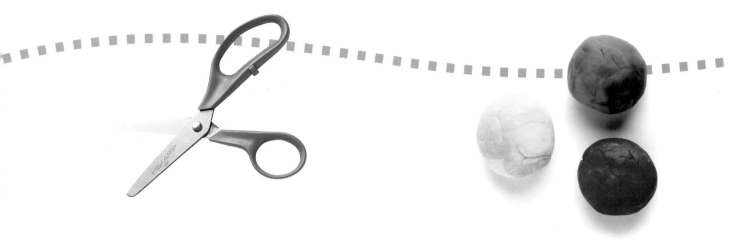

Published in 2009 by The Rosen Publishing Group Inc.
29 East 21st Street, New York, NY 10010

Copyright © 2009 Wayland/The Rosen Publishing Group, Inc.

First Edition

Senior Editor: Jennifer Schofield
Designer: Jason Billin
Project maker: Anna-Marie D'Cruz
Photographer: Chris Fairclough
Proofreader: Susie Brooks

Library of Congress Cataloging-in-Publication Data

D'Cruz, Anna-Marie.
    Make your own puppets / Anna-Marie D'Cruz. — 1st ed.
        p. cm. — (Do it yourself projects)
    Includes index.
    ISBN 978-1-4358-2851-3 (library binding)
    ISBN 978-1-4358-2919-0 (paperback)
    ISBN 978-1-4358-2920-6 (6-pack)
    1. Puppet making—Juvenile literature. 2. Recycling (Waste, etc.)—
Juvenile literature. I. Title.
    TT174.7.D37 2009
    745.592'24—dc22
                                        2008033661

Manufactured in China

Acknowledgments
The Publishers would like to thank the following models:
Emel Augustin, Jade Campbell, Ammar Duffus, Akash Kohli,
Ellie Lawrence, Eloise Ramplin, and Robin Stevens

Picture Credits:
All photography by Chris Fairclough except
page 4 top Reza; Webistan/CORBIS; page 5 top Mike Segar/
Reuters/CORBIS; page 11 Richard Cummins/CORBIS

Note to parents and teachers:
The projects in this book are designed to be made by children. However, we do recommend adult supervision at all times since the Publisher cannot be held responsible for any injury caused while making the projects.

Contents

All about puppets

A puppet is an object that is "brought to life" with the use of hands, rods, or strings. People who work puppets are known as puppeteers.

PUPPETS LONG AGO

Puppets have been used for thousands of years to entertain and also to educate children. Many styles of puppet have developed from different cultures around the world.

Some of the first puppets, which were used in religious festivals, were like masks with opening and closing mouths. Another early form of puppet, believed to have started in China, is the shadow puppet (see above right). This is a flat-shaped puppet moved by rods and lit from behind. A shadow is cast onto a screen in front of an audience.

TYPES OF PUPPETS

Today, there are many types of puppet and they can range in size from small puppets that fit on your fingers or hands, to rod puppets (see left) that the puppeteer moves with sticks. Japanese Bunraku puppets are so big that they need three people to work them.

FAMOUS PUPPETS

Throughout history, some puppets have become famous. Often, puppets created for children become popular with adults, too.

Punch and his wife Judy have been delighting audiences since the 1600s. The story of Pinocchio, written by the Italian author, Carlo Collodi, has been a children's favorite since the late 1800s. Pinocchio is a marionette—a puppet that is controlled with strings by the puppeteer—that comes to life. Other popular puppets include the Muppets, with the well-loved characters Kermit the Frog (see above left) and Miss Piggy.

GET STARTED

Puppets can be made from all types of things, such as paper plates, paper bags, empty paper towel tubes, and old socks. In this book, you can discover how to make many different types of puppets. Try to use materials that you already have, either at home or at school. Reusing and recycling materials like this is good for the environment and it will also save you money. The projects in this book have all been made and decorated, but do not worry if yours look a little different—just have fun making and playing with your puppets.

Venus flytrap

The Venus flytrap is a flesh-eating plant. Its leaves trap insects by snapping shut as the insects land on them. The plant's digestive juices turn the insect into mush that the plant can eat. Follow these steps to make your own flesh-eating flytrap puppet.

1 Cover your work surface with a few layers of newspaper. Paint the inside of the plate red and allow it to dry. Fold the plate in half.

2 Curl the small strip of card around your thumb, to make a hoop through which your thumb fits. Tape the ends together. Do the same with the longer strip, this time curling it around your hand. Make sure it fits around four fingers. The hoops will be used to open and close the puppet.

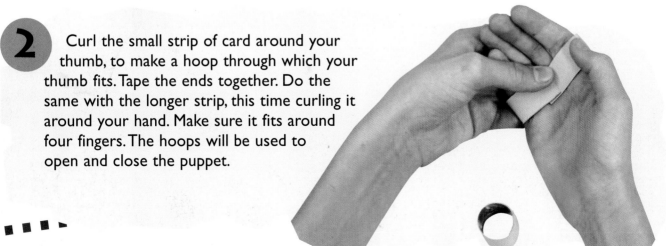

3 Use double-sided tape to attach one hoop to each half of the plate. Paint the hoops and the outside of the plate green, and allow them to dry.

4 Staple the straws around the edge of one half of the plate and bend them upward.

5 Attach more "teeth" to the other half of the plate so that when the trap is closed, they fall between the ones on the other half of the plate.

6 Place your thumb and fingers in the hoops to open and close the flytrap. What other kind of character do you think this puppet could be?

MEAT EATERS

Flesh-eating or carnivorous plants, such as the Venus flytrap and pitcher plant, grow in swamps where there are not enough nutrients in the soil. They catch and eat small insects to make sure they get all the nutrients they need to live.

Safari fingers

Finger puppets are easy to use. They sit on the ends of your fingers. Bring them to life by placing them on your middle finger and wriggling your fingertips.

YOU WILL NEED

compass
various colored sheets
   of thin card or paper
pencil
pair of scissors
tape
glue
felt-tip pens

FOR THE LION

1 Using a compass, draw a circle on your card that is 5½ in. (14cm) in diameter. Cut it out and fold it into four. Cut out the quarters.

2 Curl a quarter around your finger to make a cone shape. Tape it together so that one straight edge overlaps the other straight edge.

3 Draw around the open end of the cone on a piece of colored paper. Use this circle as a guide and draw a mane, as shown. Cut it out.

4 Hold the mane over the open end of the cone and stick it down to the inside using small strips of tape.

5 To finish the lion, draw the eyes and ears or cut them out from colored paper. Color in the nose with a felt-tip pen.

FOR THE RHINOCEROS

Repeat the first two steps from the lion instructions, but use different-colored paper.

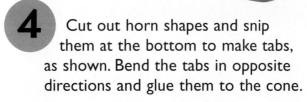

3 Cut ear shapes from colored paper and stick them to the cone.

4 Cut out horn shapes and snip them at the bottom to make tabs, as shown. Bend the tabs in opposite directions and glue them to the cone.

5 To finish your rhino, draw eyes or cut them out from colored paper and stick them on.

FOR THE GAZELLE

Repeat the first two steps from the lion instructions, but use different-colored paper.

3 Cut ear shapes from colored paper and stick them to the cone.

4 For the horns, cut out strips of paper. Wrap them around a pencil to make them curl. Stick the ends of the horns to the inside of the cone.

ENDANGERED RHINOS

Like many wild animals, the rhinoceros is endangered. In fact, the black rhino is disappearing faster than any other large animal on Earth. Unless rhinos are protected from the people who hunt them, they will become extinct.

5 Draw eyes or cut them out from colored paper and glue them on. Color in the nose with a felt-tip pen.

.. Creepy crawly caterpillar

The caterpillar is slow-crawling insect. Its body is made up of segments that squash up and stretch out as it moves along. Follow the steps to make this simple caterpillar rod puppet.

YOU WILL NEED

green and yellow colored paper

pair of scissors

glue

small wooden sticks

large pom-pom

2 stick-on eyes

small pom-pom

2 popsicle sticks

1 Cut a strip of green paper 1 x 22 in. (2.5 x 56cm) long. You may need to glue a few strips together depending on the size of paper you use. Do the same with the yellow paper.

2 Place the strips at right angles to each other, so that they look like an "L.." Glue the ends together. Fold the strips of paper over each other until you reach the end. Cut off any extra paper and glue the ends together.

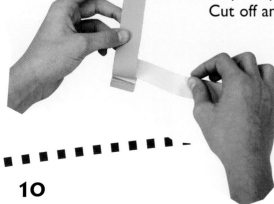

3 To make antennae, glue small wooden sticks to one end of the paper spring. When the glue has dried, add a large pom-pom to make the caterpillar's head. Glue on eyes and a small pom-pom for the nose.

LIFE CYCLES

The caterpillar is one stage in the life cycle of a butterfly. The cycle begins with the butterfly laying eggs, which hatch into caterpillars. When a caterpillar is ready to change, it forms a chrysalis, from which the butterfly emerges.

4 Glue a popsicle stick between the folds in the paper near the head. Glue the other stick near the tail end.

5 To make the caterpillar move, hold the sticks and move the back one toward the front one, then move the front one forward.

Scary shark

Decorating a sock is an easy way to make a puppet. Your hand and arm give the puppet movement. Here is a great way of using an old or odd sock to make a fierce puppet.

YOU WILL NEED

1 clean old sock
felt-tip pens
2 stick-on eyes
double-sided tape
sheet of white card,
    4 x 6 in. (10 x 16cm)
pencil
pair of scissors
piece of gray card,
    2¾ x 2½ in.
    (7 x 6cm)

1   Put the sock over the hand you do not use to write with. Put your thumb into the heel of the sock to make the bottom of the shark's mouth. Use a felt-tip pen to mark where you want to put the eyes, gills, and fin.

2   Take off the sock and draw on the nose and gills. Tape on the eyes with small pieces of double-sided tape, one on either side of what will be the head.

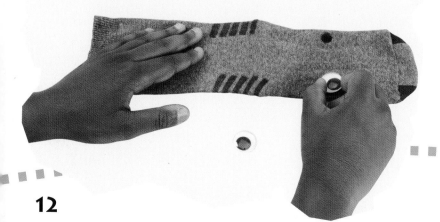

SHARK FACTS

Sharks are fish. Like all fish, they take in oxygen from the water using gills instead of lungs. Sharks have an amazing sense of smell—more than half a shark's brain helps it to smell!

3 On the white card, draw a mouth and teeth using the picture below as a guide. Cut it out.

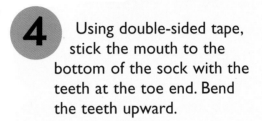

4 Using double-sided tape, stick the mouth to the bottom of the sock with the teeth at the toe end. Bend the teeth upward.

5 On the gray card, draw a fin shape as shown. Fold the card along the dotted line. Cut out the fin and snip the bottom of the fin down the middle, up to the fold line. Fold the two halves in opposite directions to make tabs. Tape the fin to the top of the sock with double-sided tape.

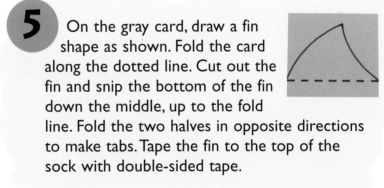

6 The puppet is ready to try on! As you put the sock on, carefully fold the mouth where it naturally wants to bend. Can you make it look as though the shark is swimming in the sea?

Pirate shadows

A shadow puppet is usually a flat shape and is moved with rods or sticks. A light is shone behind the puppet to cast a shadow onto a screen. The audience sits in front of the screen to watch the shadows. Make your own pirate puppet and put on a show.

YOU WILL NEED

sheet of card
pencil
pair of scissors
pen
6 paper fasteners
3 long popsicle sticks

1 Copy the shapes shown onto card and cut them out. Label the pieces and use a pen to mark the circles shown on the card. This is where the holes need to go. Ask an adult to help you to push the pencil through the marks to make small holes.

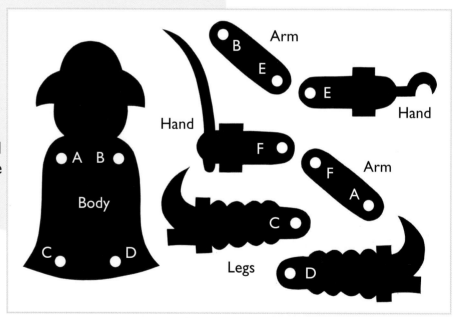

2 To make the arms, push a paper fastener through the arm piece holes labelled F and E. Then add the hands, joining hand F to the F hole and hand E to the E hole. Open out the paper fastener.

14

SHADOWS

A shadow is made when light is blocked. Light travels in straight lines, so it cannot go around an object and it cannot travel through objects, unless they are in some way see-through. Since the light cannot light up the area behind the object, it forms the shadow.

3 Use paper fasteners to attach the arms to the shoulder part of the body, joining hole A to hole A and hole B to hole B.

4 In the same way, attach both legs (C and D) to the bottom of the body.

5 Tape the popsicle sticks to the back of the puppet on the hands and one up the middle.

6 Using the middle stick, hold the pirate in the air. Wiggle the sticks attached to the hands to see how the puppet can move. Try hanging a sheet up between two chairs with a lamp behind you. Use the sheet as a screen for your puppet show.

Wizard glove

Glove puppets sit over the hand. Some are simple and have no arms or legs, like the sock puppet. Others have arms that are moved by the thumb and little finger. Make your own wizard glove puppet to create some magic.

YOU WILL NEED

paper

pencil

pair of scissors

different colored felt

foam sheet

craft glue

needle

thread

card or paper for eyes

felt-tip pens

yarn for beard and eyebrows

foil stars

1 Draw an outline of your hand on the paper. Make sure your thumb and little finger stick out.

2 Draw a simple person shape around the outline, making it about 1¾ in. (2cm) larger all the way around. Round off the top to give a good head shape. Cut out the shape so that you have a template.

3 Draw around the template on your felt and cut two pieces the same shape to give you a front and a back piece.

GET SEWING

To sew a running stitch, thread a needle and tie a knot at one end of the thread. Push the point of the needle down through the fabric. Bring the needle back up again at a point farther forward from where you went down. Repeat to give a row of stitches that look the same on both sides of the fabric.

4 Cut out hands for your puppet from a foam sheet and glue them to the back of one of the body shapes. This is the back of your wizard.

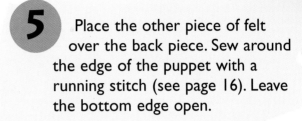

5 Place the other piece of felt over the back piece. Sew around the edge of the puppet with a running stitch (see page 16). Leave the bottom edge open.

6 Cut out a circle of the foam sheet for the head and glue it onto the front of the puppet. Draw eyes on some card, cut them out, and glue them on. Add a beard and eyebrows by gluing on short pieces of yarn. Cut a nose and a mouth from foam and stick them on, too.

7 Make a hat by sewing two triangles of felt up the sides. Glue the hat to the top of the head. Use stars to decorate the wizard's outfit. When all the glue has dried, your puppet is ready to bring to life.

Chinese dragon

Dragon puppets are used in dances as part of Chinese New Year festivals. The dragons have a large head and a long tail. They are held up on sticks and carried by lots of people. Follow the steps to make your own dragon.

YOU WILL NEED

compass
pencil
colored card
pair of scissors
needle
25 mini cupcake cups
28 in. (70cm) thick thread
tape
colored card for the head,
  8 x 5½ in. (20 x 14cm)
felt-tip pens
double-sided tape
2 chopsticks

1 Use the compass to draw 26 circles that are 2½ in. (6cm) across on the colored card. Cut out the circles.

2 Ask an adult to help you pierce holes through the centers of the circles with a needle. Pierce holes in the center of the bottoms of the cupcake cups, too.

CHINESE NEW YEAR

In China, new year celebrations last for fifteen days at the end of January or the beginning of February. People's homes are colorfully decorated and a feast of traditional foods is prepared. The fifteenth day of the new year is marked with the Lantern Festival.

3 Knot one end of the thread. Thread the unknotted end through the hole in the center of one circle, and pull the thread through to the knot. Stick some tape over the knot to stop it slipping through the hole.

4 Thread on a cupcake cup and another circle. Repeat this until you have used all the circles. Finish with a circle. Knot the thread and cut off any that is spare. Stick a piece of tape over the knot.

5 Draw a dragon's head on the card and color it in. Cut it out. Cut a slit on the neck to make tabs to stick the head to one end of your dragon.

6 Draw a tail tip out of card and cut it out. Cut a slit at the bottom to make tabs. Fold the tabs in opposite directions. Stick the tail tip to the other end of the dragon.

7 Tape a chopstick to the back of the head and another to the back of the tail.

8 The puppet is now ready to use. Move the rods and see if you can make the dragon rise and fall. It will make a great rustling sound, too!

Robot marionette

Marionette puppets are moved by string or wires that are attached to the arms, legs, and head of the puppet. The puppeteer controls the puppet by moving a wooden bar attached to the other end of the strings or wires.

1 From the tube, cut pieces that are 4 in. (10cm), 2 in. (5cm), 1¾ in. (4.5cm), and 1¼ in. (3cm) long. The two longer pieces will make the head and body of the robot, and the shorter ones will be used for the feet and arms.

2 Take the two shorter rolls and cut each one in half to give you four arcs.

3 Roll each arc into a smaller tube and staple the ends together. The smaller ones will become the feet and the longer ones, the arms. Cover your work surface with newspaper and paint all the tubes silver.

4 Using two of the longer strips of colored card, staple one end of each to the feet of the robot and the other to the bottom of the body. Do the same with the two shorter pieces, attaching the arms to the sides at the top of the body.

5 To attach the head, staple the last strip of card from front to back at the top of the body to make a curve. Staple the head tube to the top of the curved card.

6 Make a cross with the popsicle sticks, holding them together with the rubber bands.

7 Pierce a hole in the middle of the top of the head with a needle. Pass the 10 in. (25cm) piece of thread through it. Knot it and stick it to the inside of the tube. Tie the other end around the middle of the crossbar.

8 Pierce a hole in the middle of the arms and legs. Knot the ends of each of the four remaining threads. Pass the two longer threads through the holes in the legs, and the shorter ones through the holes in the arms. Tie the other ends to the crossbar, with the threads to the legs at the front. Tie them so that when the puppet is hanging, the threads are not too loose.

9 Add pieces of colored card and stick-on eyes to decorate the head and body. Hold up the crossbar. Move it backward and forward and from side to side, to see if you can make your robot walk and flap its arms up and down.

Glossary

antennae

The feelers on the head of an insect.

carnivorous

Animals, such as lions, and plants, such as the Venus flytrap, that eat meat.

chrysalis

The hard cover a caterpillar makes around itself before it turns into a butterfly.

digestive juices

The substances that soften and break down food, inside an animal or plant.

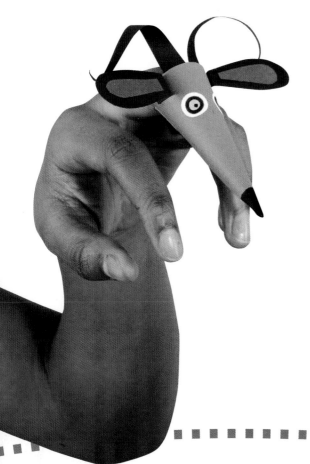

endangered

When there are very few of a certain kind of animal left in the wild. For example, the rhinoceros and the tiger are both endangered.

extinct

When there are no more of a certain animal left anywhere in the world. For example, dinosaurs are extinct.

gills

The parts of a fish's body that it uses to breathe.

life cycle

The stages in an animal or plant's life. The caterpillar is one stage in the life cycle of a butterfly or moth.

nutrients

Foods or substances that give animals and plants the things they need to stay alive.

oxygen

One of the gases in air that people and all other animals need to breathe in to stay alive. Fish and many other animals found in water get their oxygen from the water instead of air.

protect

To stop something from being harmed or killed. When animals are protected, there are laws that say what can and cannot be done to the animals.

puppeteer
The person who controls a puppet.

recycling
To recycle something is to change it or treat it, so that it can be used again.

reusing
Using something for a different purpose. For example, if you use the cardboard from a cereal box to make a project, you are reusing the cardboard.

swamp
Land that it very wet and often very muddy. Swamps are sometimes called marshes.

tabs
Flaps or small pieces that stick out of something.

traditional
Things that have existed for a long time or that have been passed down through families.

FURTHER INFORMATION

BOOKS TO READ

Making Shadow Puppets
by Jill Bryant
(Kids Can Press, 2002)

Puppet Planet
by John Kennedy
(North Light Books, 2006)

WEB SITES

Due to the changing nature of Internet links, PowerKids Press has developed an online list of Web sites related to the subject of this book. This site is updated regularly. Please use this link to access this list:
www.powerkidslinks.com/diyp/puppets

Index